The Mindful Lifestyle

By
GARY GREEN

Strategic Book Publishing and Rights Co.

Dedication

This book is dedicated to all who want their lives to be better, regardless of social standing, economic class, race, religion, political party, gender, sexual orientation, age, nationality, or any other way people can be grouped together. We are more alike than we are different. May you all find the peace that dwells within.

Acknowledgments

I want to acknowledge all the mindfulness teachers going back to the beginning of time who, through compassion, have sought to help the rest of us access the Divine Truth that resides in us all. My gratitude to you all.

Contents

Preface

Mindfulness is all the rage these days. It is easy to see why. There has been a lot of research to determine what, if any, the benefits of regular mindfulness practice are. In fact, the National Institute of Health's National Library of Medicine lists over twenty thousand mindfulness studies. Some of the benefits listed in "5-Minute Health Fixes," by the doctors from *The Doctors* TV show, include:

- Reduced chronic stress

- Pain management

- Reduced blood levels of cortisol, a stress hormone linked to early cognitive decline and other chronic health issues

- Improved functioning of the adrenal glands

- Reduced heart and respiration rate

- Lower blood pressure

- Reduced insomnia

- Improved immune system functioning

- Improved antibody response to the flu vaccine

- Increased energy

- Reduced gastrointestinal upset

- Improved anger management and reduction in depression and anxiety

- Reduction of repetitive, ruminating thoughts

- Increased empathy

- Improved attention and ability to stay on task

- Reduced judgmental thinking

- Enhanced ability to quickly refocus after being distracted

- Thickened cerebral cortex, the brain region linked to planning and regulating emotions

- Reduced automatic emotional reactivity, such as angry outbursts or anxiety attacks

- Increased grey matter and growth in the size of the brain

Is mindfulness a fad that will pass in time, or is it a tool that will be integrated into our society for the betterment of all? I certainly hope it is the latter.

My experience in using mindfulness techniques to recover from depression and alcoholism tells me that mindfulness practice can trigger many positive changes in a person's life. In addition to the techniques themselves, there are some concepts associated with mindfulness that have helped me to make positive changes to my life. These positive changes continue even today, though I have been sober for over twenty years and my depression is a thing of the past. This tells me that a person doesn't have to be sick to benefit from mindfulness.

My experience in teaching mindfulness techniques and concepts to mentally ill and chemically dependent adults tells me, through the changes I have seen in others, that mindfulness has broad application for many people. It also tells me that teaching these principles requires a simple, no-nonsense approach.

That is what you will find here. In writing this book, I hope that some of the people who read it will use these principles to improve the quality of their lives and relationships.

I will draw on a wide range of sources to give the reader a solid understanding of mindfulness. I am aware that I will be saying some things here that some "experts" will disagree with, such as my inclusion of certain practices under the umbrella of mindfulness. I believe that including what I have will make the practice of mindfulness easier to understand.

There is one more thing I will mention. Throughout this book I use the word recovery a lot. This is because of my experience with recovery and my work helping others with their recovery. I believe that what we generally refer to as "recovery" is a structured, accelerated growth and development that mirrors the growth and development that everyone experiences throughout their lifespan. Your life may be humming along just the way you want. Good for you. You will still benefit from living the mindful lifestyle.

Chapter 1
Transcendental Meditation

Anytime a person is considering a lifestyle change, there has to be a starting place. I think a good place to start the discussion of mindful lifestyle is where I started: Transcendental Meditation (TM).

Transcendental Meditation is the type of mindfulness practice perhaps most familiar to Western society. This is because several individuals, particularly the Maharishi Mahesh Yogi, popularized TM starting in the late 1960s. People really took notice when he taught TM to the Beatles. He developed a large organization to teach the technique that reached even to rural central Minnesota, where I lived at the time.

I first learned about TM in my early twenties. At the time I was a depressed alcoholic, but I thought the troubles I was having were primarily due to stress. I was having trouble sleeping, difficulty concentrating, and a lot of anxiety, all of which was contributing to my difficulties with alcohol. In addition, I was dealing with a lot of fatigue, which I assumed was related to the sleep difficulties, and chronic heartburn, which our family doctor said was more about what I was thinking than what I was eating. "It's not what you're eating, it's what's eating you."

Armed with those words of wisdom, I began my search for knowledge about stress. What I found was the work of Hans Selye, one of the pioneers of stress research. He defined stress as "the non-specific response of the body to any demand made upon it." Or, to put it another way, the body reacts to perceived "threats" by getting ready to run away or to fight—the fight-or-flight reaction. These threats, by the way, are generally some kind of change in our environment. Because change is inevitable, it would seem that we constantly experience stressors. This reaction is typified by increased heart rate and respiration, increased blood pressure, and the release of adrenaline and other stress hormones. It is easy to see how such a reaction is useful when presented with real threats, such as a lion stalking one of our ancestors on the African plain. We see the lion and run away. We are able to run faster because of the stress reaction. However, it should be noted that pleasant things as well as unpleasant things can trigger the stress reaction. In addition, there are many factors in modern life, such as climate change, that are constant and not easily dealt with. Lack of stimulation, or boredom, can also be a source of stress. But it is important to remember in all cases that it is not the stressor but our reaction to it that causes the problem. The result is a chronic "biological stress syndrome" that is a factor in most of the health problems we have, from high blood pressure to mental illness. I had stress symptoms in abundance.

Exercise is touted as an effective way to deal with stress. After all, stress is basically the body's fight-or-flight reaction, so exercise is the most "natural" way to deal with it. The problem with exercise is that if you are depressed, it is difficult to make yourself do it. It is somewhat ironic that later studies found that exercise can be as effective as antidepressant medication.

Fortunately for me, there are things other than exercise that are effective in reducing the impact of stress in our lives. There is something called the "relaxation response," which is typified by lower heart rate and respiration, reduced muscle tension, lower blood pressure, and reduced levels of the stress hormones mentioned above. Transcendental Meditation is touted as an effective way to trigger the relaxation response. We all know that the effects of regular exercise carry over from one session to the next. Regular exercise makes us fit and more physically able between sessions. Similarly, the effects of regular meditation carry over into the rest of our lives, making us more relaxed in general. And, just as with exercise, the effects are cumulative. We now know that regular mindfulness practice can change the actual structure of the brain.

Initially I was somewhat reluctant to learn and practice the TM technique because my perception was that it was part of the Hindu religion. I did not want to convert. However, I learned that TM is not a religious ritual but instead simply a mental exercise. I have since learned that every religious tradition uses mindfulness practice in some form.

The basics of TM are simple. Sit quietly with your eyes closed and repeat your "mantra" to yourself for fifteen or twenty minutes. A mantra is a word or phrase that is repeated either aloud or to yourself as a mindfulness practice. As with any other mindfulness practice, when other thoughts pop into your head, notice them, let them go, and gently direct your attention back to your mantra.

A mantra can be anything. If you use a phrase, make it short. Research indicates that mantras that have spiritual meaning to *you* are most effective in achieving the relaxation response, but even nonsense words are acceptable. Avoid mantras that have negative connotations for you. When I learned TM, the teacher said that your mantra must be given to you by your guru (i.e., teacher). I don't know that that is true, but I don't believe the Maharishi's were deliberately deceptive. I think that is just part of the tradition. I still use the mantra that was given to me. It is a Sanskrit word, but I do not speak Sanskrit, so I have no idea what it means. But it still works. I believe it is perfectly acceptable to pick your own.

If you are ready to try, here is an exercise: First you must pick your mantra, following the guidelines above. When you have chosen your mantra, sit comfortably with your feet flat on the floor and your eyes closed. Then start repeating your mantra to yourself quietly (in your head or aloud). When your mind wanders, gently direct your attention back to your mantra. Do this for fifteen minutes. You may use a timer or check a clock. I used to hold my wristwatch in my hands and check it. It did not take long before I was able to meditate for exactly the allotted time without looking. Or you could just guess—close is good enough. After fifteen minutes have passed, stop repeating your mantra and open your eyes. It is not a good idea to jump right up afterward. You are coming out of a deeply relaxed state, so you should give your body a couple of minutes to adjust.

So what did you notice? Most people experience deep relaxation. If all you got from mindfulness practice was this deep relaxation, it would still be well worth the effort. This is because, as mentioned above, the effects of the session carry over into the rest of your day—and the effects are cumulative. That means that over time most beginners find that they are more relaxed in general. This is a good thing because the effects of stress are cumulative as well. So if stress is giving you high blood pressure, regular meditation will help lower it. If stress is making you generally anxious, regular meditation will help. In fact, relaxation techniques are pretty standard in the treatment of anxiety disorders.

Other things you may notice include:

1. Some people notice twitching, especially in the arms and legs but also in the face. My teacher explained that this is chronic muscle tension releasing. While this can be distracting, it is not a serious problem. It often goes away with regular meditation. I have found that consciously tensing then releasing the muscles that are twitching is helpful.

2. Some people notice a "spinning" sensation or see in their mind's eye a swirling shape like a galaxy. This is not a problem either. Notice it and then gently direct your attention back to your mantra. I don't know what this sensation is, but I have experienced it for years without coming into apparent harm.

3. You will notice that thoughts pop into your head. They may be random or there may be a theme. Perhaps you have some pressing issues in your life and have recurring thoughts about them. In fact, many beginners think that if they have intrusive thoughts, that means they can't meditate. Nothing could be further from the truth. One of the brain's jobs is to generate thoughts. It does this 24/7, so it makes sense that it would continue to do it while you are meditating. When thoughts pop up, just notice them and let go of them. Then gently direct your attention back to your mantra. I have noticed over the years that my thoughts still pop up during meditation, but they seem to come further apart.

4. I have seen beginning meditators get quite upset over distractions. When I was teaching mindfulness, I would tell people that it is impossible to do mindfulness practice without distractions because most of them come from your own mind, as mentioned above. Learning how to handle distractions is part of learning mindfulness

practices. The best way to deal with distractions of any kind is to notice them and then let them go, gently returning your attention to your mantra (or whatever mindfulness practice you are doing). If the distraction is something you must attend to, then attend to it. You can return to your session later if possible. Try to not get too upset over it. Having said that, I will suggest that, at least in the beginning, you find a relatively quiet place to do your regular meditation.

If you miss a session, it is not the end of the world. But try not to make a habit of it. The maximum benefit comes from regular, consistent practice. When I first started, I was told to meditate twice a day for twenty minutes each time—and to try to make it the same time each day. I was also told that if I was extra tired or had to work late, I could do an extra session. The same goes for being sick: if you get a cold or the flu, meditate as much as you can. The deep rest helps your body fight the germs and heal. I have tried this, and I believe it does shorten the cold's duration.

I have noticed beginning meditators concerned about falling asleep while meditating. All it means when you fall asleep while meditating is that you need more sleep. If you regularly fall asleep while doing mindfulness practice, I suggest you take a serious look at your sleep habits and work on your sleep hygiene. When people start to meditate regularly, they may find (as I did) that they need more sleep initially. This is probably because they haven't been getting enough. Current research indicates that most Americans do not get enough sleep. This leads to a cumulative fatigue. If you find yourself in this situation, simply continue to meditate regularly and this should stabilize, as it did for me. In fact, most people who meditate regularly find they feel more rested on less than the recommended eight hours of sleep than they ever did before they started meditating.

While it is not a big deal if you doze off once in a while, you don't want to make a regular habit of it. It was not unusual for me to see my clients heading for the morning mindfulness practice with a pillow under one arm and a blanket under the other. Their intent was to use meditation time to catch a little nap. I discouraged this practice in my clients and I discourage it here. If you need more sleep, get more sleep. Meditation time is different.

Another possibility is that you may find repeating a mantra over and over to be quite boring. This is not unusual and is actually part of the process. Again, just notice the feeling and let it go. Gently return your attention to your mantra. Persistence pays off. You'll just have to trust me on this one—or, better yet, find out for yourself.

There is another aspect of changing your routine by inserting a "spiritual" practice like meditating into your daily routine. If you find that others react negatively to it or try to discourage you, my advice would be to acknowledge their concerns but persist in your plan to change. Good friends will accept such positive efforts. People who persist in their attempts to interfere with your plans are probably sapping your energy in other ways as well.

So what actually happens during a session? The Maharishi's organization uses the analogy that the mind is like a body of water. When we are in our regular conscious state, we are at the surface. It is our attention to external stimuli and internal events like thoughts that keep us at that surface level. Or, put another way, there is a Hindu saying that the mind is like a tree full of chattering monkeys, each one demanding our attention. It is listening to the chatter that keeps us at our normal level of consciousness. As we direct our attention to our mantra and away from the chattering, we gradually sink to the bottom of the water.

The bottom represents "Infinite Intelligence." What Infinite Intelligence means may be open to some interpretation. Some might believe that it represents contact with the Infinite or Higher Power. I cannot verify this. However, we do know that there are measurable changes to the electrical activity in the brain that would tend to indicate a more relaxed state. We also know that, when practicing TM, the tissue connecting the two halves of the brain (the corpus callosum) greatly increases its electrical activity. Apparently the left, or logical, hemisphere of the cerebellum and the right, or emotional/intuitive hemisphere, are "talking" to each other more than they do in our normal conscious state. This could have some implications later when we are discussing the concept of "Wise Mind." As you relax there are physical changes as well. Respiration, heart rate, blood pressure, and stress hormones in the blood all decrease.

Essentially we are learning to ignore the chattering monkeys. Or perhaps we learn to recognize thoughts for what they are: sometimes random and possessing only the power we choose to give them.

My suggestion would be that after reading this chapter you put this book down and find time to fit two twenty-minute sessions of TM into your day. If you can't find twenty minutes, you can get by with less, but I wouldn't do less than ten. I suggest once in the morning and once before supper. I suggest you do this for a week before continuing with the rest of the book.

Chapter 2
What Is Mindfulness?

Now that you have had some experience with a mindfulness practice, let's talk a bit about what mindfulness is and how to incorporate it into your lifestyle.

I invite you to take a moment to sit quietly and notice everything about that moment. Notice your surroundings—the sights, the sounds, the smells. Notice how you feel—any muscle tension or pain. Are you hungry or thirsty? Breathe normally, but notice your breath as it comes and goes. Thoughts will come into your awareness. Notice them and let them pass through. Most important, if any of your thoughts are judgmental, let them go. Pause your reading to do this exercise for a minute or two or as long as you like, then return to reading.

That is the essence of mindfulness—a moment and all it contains. It has been my experience that most present moments are okay, even pleasant.

Mindfulness has been around for thousands of years. Some form of mindfulness has been incorporated into every major religion or spiritual tradition. In recent years mindfulness and mindfulness practice have emerged in many areas of the mainstream, from education to the military. Perhaps the strongest impact has been in the areas of mental health and chemical health. Mindfulness has been demonstrated to be effective in reducing anxiety and depression, improving concentration, and improving sleep habits. In recent years mindfulness practice has been added to treatment regimens across a wide range of mental and physical health diagnostic categories. In fact, it has been demonstrated that regular mindfulness practice actually changes the physical structure of the brain.

Furthermore, because of the associated relaxation response, mindfulness practice has demonstrated usefulness in treatment of any physical disorder that has a stress component, which is most of them.

So what is mindfulness? One possible definition: mindfulness is awareness of what *is*, without judgment, through direct and immediate experience. Another way to put it: paying attention on purpose or directing your attention to just one thing—this present moment.

Mindfulness practice, then, is the repeated act of directing your awareness to just one thing—the present moment. Many people think that mindfulness practice is difficult when they first start. In fact, many people don't like it at first. However, most people find that if they stick with it long enough to experience some of the benefits, they *really* like it.

One of the things that causes people to think they can't do it is that random thoughts pop into their head after they start mindfulness practice. What they don't realize is that this happens to everybody. The proper thing to do at this point is to gently direct your attention back to the mindfulness practice. These mental intrusions will happen less often with practice. Mindfulness is a skill, and like any skill it improves with practice.

Another important point to remember is to use the proper words. Stay away from words like "focus" and "concentrate." Instead say, "direct your attention." Words like focus and concentrate imply more effort than you should be using. Improvement is attained by repetition and not intensity of effort.

Mindfulness practices can be divided into three basic categories: observation, participation, and description. I realize that there other systems of organizing mindfulness or meditative practices. For example, a recent *Scientific American* article uses the categories of focused attention, mindfulness, and compassion and loving kindness. My problem with this system is that focused attention is simply directing your attention to one thing—the very definition of mindfulness. Compassion is an attitude that grows out of regular mindfulness practice, as I will explain in depth in chapter 7. Using the categories of observation, participation, and description makes the most sense in pursuing the mindful lifestyle, as I will explain below.

Observation means directing your attention to direct sensory experience without evaluation. You can observe anything your senses can detect. Common types of observation include listening to music, observing your breath, observing a piece of food in your mouth, and more. The idea is to direct your attention to the sensation and let any thoughts that come into your awareness drift right out of it again.

In fact, you can make an exercise of observing your thoughts. Just sit quietly with your eyes closed. As thoughts come into your awareness, notice them. Don't evaluate them, just notice and let them go. Some people use a visualization to help with the letting go. I have used the visualization that thoughts are balloons. I notice them and let go of their strings, and they float away. I suppose what is really happening here is that, because you can only think of one thing at a time, directing your attention to the visualization (a balloon, in this case) forces you to think about the balloon and not whatever the original thought was. Anyway, if you are engaging in the mindfulness practice of observing your thoughts, pick a visualization—for instance, thoughts as cars in a slowly moving train, clouds floating by, boats floating down a river, horses walking by, or whatever you want. Any image will work as long as it is something that naturally moves. This can be a useful exercise because it can trigger the relaxation response and can demonstrate that thoughts are just thoughts.

My thoughts are something I own. They have no more power over me than I choose to give them. You might think this is a bold statement coming from a recovering alcoholic; it is well known in the recovery community that "willpower" is not an effective way to become sober. However, I have observed that thinking about drinking is not what causes urges, but rather the other way around. Urges cause thoughts, which in turn feed the urges and make them stronger. In this regard, thinking about *not* doing something is the same as thinking about doing it. Best to direct your attention elsewhere and let your unhealthy urges wither on the vine.

However, I would avoid this exercise if you are feeling an intense emotion about something. Strong emotions tend to influence what you think about, and thinking about whatever triggered the strong emotions can prolong or increase the intensity—which will not trigger the relaxation response. If you find yourself in this situation, I suggest you try practices that fit into the participation category as described in the next section.

After I have used this exercise in class, I generally ask students if they notice where their thoughts come from or where they go. I have gotten some interesting answers, but after some discussion all classes have come to the same conclusion: thoughts come from your subconscious or unconscious mind, enter your awareness or conscious mind, and then return to your subconscious. While this seems like kind of a no-brainer when you think about it, it does demonstrate two important things:

1. Thoughts are real things that we can pick up or put down at will. They are something that we have. While we do have a lot of control over which thoughts we are currently aware of, there can also be a random element. This is particularly noticeable when we are doing a mindfulness practice such as TM. Truly random thoughts pop in. That is just how our brains operate. Don't worry about it.

2. We are not our thoughts. In one sense everything within our skin is us. The essence of who we really are is something else. We know this at some level. Just look at our language. We say *my* body, *my* brain, *my* mind, and *my* thoughts. So who are *we*? We are the observers, and, to paraphrase a former president, we are the *deciders*. So why do we care about that? What's the big deal? Well, the big deal is that if you are looking at your life and want to change some things, you can—if you learn how.

I will list a few of the many observation mindfulness practices here:

1. Sit comfortably and place a piece of chocolate on your tongue. Close your eyes and observe everything you can about the chocolate without eating it. You may have to swallow some saliva. That's okay. As with any other

21

mindfulness practice, notice your thoughts and let them go—especially any thoughts you have about chewing or swallowing the chocolate. The chocolate will dissolve eventually. Try to make it last ten minutes. You may be wondering what benefit comes of this exercise. Well, you are learning the skill of not responding to your urges. Perhaps if you have urges that trouble you (overeating, excessive drinking, etc.), this could be a tool to help you control those urges. However, if you are struggling with some kind of addiction, you should know that this is not the whole answer; it is just one of many tools you should have in your toolbox.

2. Select one of the many relaxation CDs available. Really, it could be any relaxing music. Sit comfortably and listen to it for twenty minutes or so. You may be wondering at this point what makes mindful listening different from regular listening. The difference is that with mindful listening you ignore everything else. Notice thoughts that pop into your mind and then direct your attention back to the music.

3. Find a peaceful place in nature. Sit comfortably and notice your senses—all of them. Don't strain any particular sense. Just notice what they all are telling you. When thoughts pop in, notice them and let them pass. Sit this way for fifteen or twenty minutes.

Participation is the act of entering completely into the activities of the moment without separating yourself from ongoing events. For example, athletes report being "in the zone" when they are playing without having to think about it. These are times when their performance is at its highest level. Singing or playing a musical instrument could be another example. People think about what they are doing during rehearsal or practice until they don't have to think about it; they just do it.

It's fine to talk about being in the zone, but we are not all high-level athletes or performers. So let's talk a little bit about skill acquisition. I'll use the example of myself learning to type. I took typing class in high school. Frankly, I was not very good. My mind wandered a lot. I was not mindful. However, even though my interest lagged, I still did all the exercises. We know that repetitive actions such as typing cause the neurons involved to become more conductive to the electrical signals needed to make the action. This means it takes less conscious effort on our part to make the same action. So when I first started learning to type, I would see an "a" and think, "Which finger is that?" I would even have to look. As I repeated the action (i.e., practiced) I remembered which finger to use and didn't have to think about that, but I still had to consciously direct my attention to the right finger. To put it another way, I was regularly directing my attention to *doing something*—typing. As I practiced more, the need for conscious direction diminished but did not go away altogether. I suspect that is because at the time my self-esteem was pretty low. I felt the need to double-check. I did not get a very good grade in typing class.

However, years later, when I returned to college at the age of twenty-eight, I was able to pick up where I had left off in high school. My self-esteem had improved enough by then that my need to double-check had diminished. I was thinking less about what I was doing; I could just direct my attention to typing. While I will never hold any speed-typing records, my typing skills are adequate to write this book, for example.

Throughout the process I was directing my attention to one thing: typing. Initially it was a slow, conscious process. Later I could just do it without thinking about it. Think of any skill you have learned. It is the same process, from walking and talking to playing a concert grand piano. It also meets the definition of mindfulness practice because you are directing your attention to one thing: the skill you are learning.

In case you were thinking that walking and talking don't count, there is such a thing as mindful walking. It could be said that people who chant their mantra aloud are talking in a mindful way.

One of the more surreal experiences in my life was chanting "om" in a large room with a few hundred mental health professionals also chanting and prominent psychologist Marsha

Linehan leading us. By the way, if you want to try this practice, say the word like this: "aaa-uuu-mmmmmmmm." Chant slowly and quietly, paying attention to everything you are experiencing while you are chanting. As always, when thoughts pop in, notice them and let them go.

One mindful walking exercise would be to simply walk in a circle, paying attention to everything about it—the physical act and sensation of walking. Another might be to walk somewhere, directing your attention not only to the act of walking but also to observing your surroundings. By the way, combining two categories like this (observation and participation) is permissible. It still counts as one practice.

You can also do mindful running. There are various ways to do this. When I have done this, I fall into a pace and my breathing sort of synchronizes with my steps—so many steps per breath. I direct my attention to doing those things. That's what makes it a mindfulness practice. There is even a Tibetan Buddhist practice called *Lung-gom*, which involves a person being able to run for days, nonstop and seemingly without fatigue. It is my understanding, however, that it takes years of training before one is able to master this technique.

In summation, I will say that anything you do can be done as a mindfulness practice by repeatedly directing your attention to what you are doing and letting your thoughts simply pass through. I will give you a few examples:

- Knitting or crocheting
- Playing a musical instrument
- Repetitive exercise
- Painting, drawing, or sculpting
- Washing dishes

The third category of mindfulness practice is *description*, which involves putting words to an observed experience. This can be either verbal or written. It can be useful for people who have difficulty identifying feelings. An important point to remember here is that you can't describe what you can't observe, such as other people's feelings. An example of description as a mindfulness practice might be writing a poem about an emotion you are feeling. I used this exercise in my mindfulness class. The good thing about poetry is that there are no rules. You can write a limerick, which does have rules, or you can do stream-of-consciousness free verse, which does not. Both are poems. Both would be an acceptable description mindfulness practice as long as you are directing all your attention to it.

While there are probably thousands of different kinds of mindfulness practices, they all fall into the three broad categories of participation, observation, and description.

When I reached this point in my class, I would ask the students if they could name anything that a person can do that would not fit into one or more of these categories. This is, of course, a trick question. I think the categories were intended to be all-inclusive. It is not a great leap of imagination at this point to say that everything a person can do can be done in a mindful way.

This brings me to my next point. Because anything a person can do can be done in a mindful way, it follows that a person can go through each day with the *intent* of being mindful as much of the time as possible. That means getting in the habit of directing your attention to the present moment. Why would you want to do that?

As I mentioned earlier, when I was doing my chores in a mindful way, I got done more quickly than when I wasn't mindful. Also, my mood was better, both while doing the chore and after I was done. This is because I could only think about one thing at a time. By directing my attention to what I was doing *at the present moment*, I wasn't spending time thinking about all the things that were wrong with my life.

Then there is the issue of daydreaming. I think that a lot of car accidents are caused by people not paying attention. For example, once my wife and I were sitting in our car in a parking lot, not moving at all. A guy backed his van right into the side of our car. Clearly he wasn't looking in the direction he was traveling—one of the basic rules of driving. If he had been driving in a mindful way, there would have been no accident and all our moods would have been better.

Or . . . I used to hate driving in traffic. I live in a rural area, but I occasionally need to drive in the Minneapolis–St. Paul area. It used to give me headaches, and I would be exhausted by the time I got to my destination. Then I discovered the joys of driving mindfully— that is, directing all my attention to the act of driving. Now I actually find myself enjoying driving in traffic. Although I'm still not an expert at this, the more I practice the better I get. I haven't had a headache from driving in years.

I think you can see from these two examples that going through the day with the intent of being mindful as much as possible has advantages. In fact, because there is so much more to mindfulness than just paying attention, it can become a lifestyle choice.

However, I wouldn't want you to think that this is a substitute for regular daily meditation.

I think this would be a good time for another exercise. Sit comfortably with your feet flat on the floor and your eyes closed. Direct all your attention to your breathing. Notice everything about it—the sensation of air filling your lungs, the sound of air moving through your nostrils, and other sensory stimuli. As you observe, count. Count to one when you breathe in, two when you breathe out, three when you breathe in, and so forth until you get to ten. Then start over. We call this exercise "counting your breath." The following list highlights things to remember when doing any mindfulness practice:

1.   You will notice after doing this for a while that random thoughts have entered your awareness. This is normal. When you notice this, gently direct your attention back to your breath. If you lose count, start over. If a noise or something else distracts you, gently direct your attention back to your breath. It is impossible to practice mindfulness without distractions because many distractions come from your own mind. Gently directing your attention back to the practice is actually what you are practicing. Distractions are irrelevant. (I know I have said some of this before, but, as a friend of mine used to say, "repetition is the cornerstone of education.")

2.   Something you will want to avoid is deciding that you can't do this because your mind wanders. It is normal for your mind to wander when you first start. Mindfulness is a skill, and like any skill it gets better with practice.

3.   Some people don't like mindfulness practice when they first try it. There are various reasons for this—from thinking it is a waste of time to discomfort with their own thoughts. Most people find that if they give it a fair chance, they really like it and it is beneficial to them.

Any kind of mindfulness practice that involves the breath is good because it connects the mind and body. Here's a simple one: Sit comfortably and close your eyes. Direct your attention to your breath. Breathe in slowly. Fill your lungs from the bottom up. Place your hands on your belly; they should move out as you fill your lungs. As you start to breathe in, start counting slowly. When your lungs are full pause, hold your breath for a few seconds and then start exhaling. Count as you exhale. Try to make the exhale last as many "counts" as the inhale. When your lungs are empty, pause again. Repeat for a few minutes, but stop if you get light-headed. You may get more oxygen than you are used to.

Another breathing exercise is one I call the "one-breath mindfulness." It can be done sitting or standing. Close your eyes and direct all your attention to your breathing. Slowly take one deep breath, pause, and then slowly let it out. As always, disregard your thoughts. Direct your attention to your breath—notice everything about it. This can be useful in calming your mind before you need to do something stressful like public speaking. While one breath can be useful, you can do more if you feel the need. Do as many as you have time to do.

There are a number of breathing exercises from yoga that are very helpful. Yoga is a broad topic, and a full treatment of it is beyond the scope of this book. I will say that hatha yoga can be an excellent way to practice mindfulness. I suggest you consult one of the many books on the subject or find a good teacher.

Chapter 3
Qualities of Mindfulness

Whereas the previous chapter discusses *what* you do when practicing mindfulness, this chapter will discuss *how* you do it.

Let's return to the definition of mindfulness: directing your attention without judgment to one thing, this present moment. This definition implies that we are going to perceive things the way they *really* are. By examining the components of this definition, we can find the qualities of mindfulness, which are *one-mindfulness*, *effectiveness*, and *nonjudgmentalness*.

Let's look at the definition without the judgment part: Directing your attention to one thing, this present moment. *One-mindfulness* is doing one thing at a time with awareness by directing your entire attention to the present moment. When you think about it, all we really have is the present moment. The past is gone and we can't change it. The future hasn't happened yet, so we don't actually have it. Many people spend so much time thinking about the past and worrying about the future that they miss out on the present. However, the present is where all the action is. It is the only time period when we can change things.

"What about planning?" you may ask. Isn't that thinking about the future? Well, obviously planning is necessary if a person is going to do anything in this life. Like any other task, planning is something you can do in a mindful way. Make your plan and then move on to something else.

Similarly, what about the past? Don't we need to learn from our past mistakes? Of course we do. Learning from the past is not the same as being stuck there. An extreme example of being stuck in the past is people with post-traumatic stress disorder (PTSD). They have experienced terrible traumatic events and regularly continue to experience the emotions that went with those events. If you happen to be one of these people, I would advise getting professional help if you haven't done so already. However, I will say that part of the treatment for PTSD is learning to leave the past in the past and live more fully in the present.

I have learned through painful experience in my life that when someone does harm to me, it actually does more harm to me than to them if I spend time ruminating on how rotten that person is and what terrible things should happen to him or her. Forgiveness is all about being in the present moment. Chronic anger is stressful and harmful to the person who carries it around. You can release that anger by making a conscious decision to release it and directing your attention to the present moment.

If you are following the mindful lifestyle, you will choose to go through each day with the intent of being fully in the present moment.

One-mindfulness also refers to doing one thing at a time. You can only really think about one thing at a time anyway. Many people believe they are thinking about several things at once, but what they are really doing is thinking different thoughts in rapid succession.

A few years back, there was a lot of talk about multitasking. It was supposed to be this great thing that would make us all more productive. Like so many things that seem too good to be true, it was. This is because you can only think of one thing at a time. If you are multitasking, you are actually bouncing your attention back and forth, which increases the chance of error. A good example would be texting and driving.

If you are following the mindful lifestyle, you will choose to do things one at a time.

Effectiveness is that quality of achieving the desired outcome from the decisions we make. All of us make decisions all day, every day. It starts when we decide to get out of bed in the morning and ends when we fall asleep at night. Many of these decisions are minor, such as what to have for lunch. Some decisions are major, such as choosing a mate or a career. Generally when we make decisions there is a desired outcome. In the case of lunch, we want it to taste good and satisfy our hunger. In the case of choosing a mate, most of us hope to be happy with our choice for a lifetime. That quality of achieving the desired outcome is called *effectiveness*.

The chances of being effective increase significantly when a person considers the "rules of the universe." For example, if we want to live a long and healthy life, we need to consider the laws of gravity and avoid stepping off cliffs whenever possible. If we want to have a tasty lunch, we must consider what we have learned about what we like to eat. When we take action based upon what we have learned, we call that using *skillful means*. The action could be anything from making a new friend using the social skills we have learned to driving a car. Everything we do involves using skills that we have learned—including mindfulness practice. No one is born with this knowledge, so it stands to reason that if we are having difficulty in a certain area, we could probably improve results if we practiced the skills needed in that area. To be most effective in achieving our desired result, we need to use skillful means.

If we are following the mindful lifestyle, we will strive to be effective by using skillful means. That means a lifetime of learning.

Nonjudgmentalness is defined as awareness of what is without assigning labels of good or evil. Many people have difficulty understanding this concept. They say, "I need my judgments." What they are referring to are evaluations. When thinking about decisions we need to make *evaluations* of the possible choices—i.e., weigh the pros and cons, etc. It only becomes judgmental thinking when we assign the labels of "good" or "evil/bad."

However, knowing the difference between pleasure and pain is not judgmental thinking. For example, a person can dislike the flavor of beets but *not* decide they are evil or morally bad.

Judgmental thinking is the basis of gender discrimination, racial bigotry, and the stigma of mental illness or addiction. Often, judgmental thinking involves the belief that certain characteristics make a person bad. So when we see those characteristics, our judgmental thinking prevents us from seeing any positive qualities the person may have. Or, to put it another way, judgmental thinking interferes with seeing who the person actually is.

People with low self-esteem, for example, have judgmental thoughts about themselves—in spite of any evidence of positive qualities. By letting go of our judgmental thoughts, we can see things as they truly are, including our own or other people's positive qualities.

Another example would be becoming romantically involved with a person based entirely on how he or she looks while ignoring any indications that the person may not be a decent person. If only it were true that a person who looks good must also be good. I have to admit that I made that mistake a few times in my youth.

Additionally, judgmental thoughts often have strong emotions attached to them. The emotional component can be either positive or negative, but it always masks reality. When a person makes decisions based primarily on emotions, the outcome is generally not what that person had hoped. In this case our decision-making is not *effective*.

Judgmental thinking and its opposite, acceptance, are an important part of living the mindful lifestyle.

People living the mindful lifestyle will strive to do one thing at a time and live fully in the present. They will strive to be effective by following the rules of the universe using skillful means. They will also strive to recognize judgmental thoughts when they arise and to release those thoughts.

Chapter 4
Acceptance

It is often said that acceptance is an essential component of recovery. In fact, the famous Serenity Prayer asks for "the serenity to accept the things I cannot change." Some people would say they are putting the cart before the horse because it is acceptance that gives a person serenity. Either way, it seems that the ability to accept things as they are is an important skill for someone wanting to work on recovery. I think it is an important skill for everybody. Certainly it is a necessary skill if you want to pursue the mindful lifestyle. To understand why this is, we must first define acceptance.

Acceptance means awareness of what is without judgment. It is the opposite of judgmental thinking. In judgmental thinking we assign labels of good and evil. With acceptance we assign no such labels. Things simply *are*. Events simply *happen*.

However, sometimes things happen that cause pain or loss of something we value. We have a tendency at these times to try to avoid the pain by rejecting the painful reality. This never works well. If a harsh reality is going to cause pain, it will cause pain whether we feel it when it happens or live in a state of denial for a while and then feel it. The truth is that pain will lessen if we allow the "natural healing process" to take place. Sometimes the reality is so harsh that we can only stand to feel the pain in small pieces. If we want to keep the healing process on track at those times, we have to remind ourselves over and over of what is actually real while letting go of our judgmental thoughts. We call this *radical acceptance*.

All this acceptance of reality sounds fine, but how do we get there from here? There are two components to the answer. The first part is recognizing and letting go of your judgmental thoughts.

Recognizing judgmental thoughts may not be as easy as you think. First I need to tell you that everyone has judgmental thoughts. I think it comes from our innate need to have a sense of belonging in a group. We tend to form those groups with people we see as similar to us. Additionally, we tend to have judgmental thoughts about anyone who is not in our group. Let me illustrate with some examples:

1. There are a lot of people in this country who, even in these "enlightened" times, believe that no African American is competent to be president of the United States—in spite of any evidence to the contrary. Racial prejudice is learned judgmental thinking that says, "My group is better than your group."

2. Think of the controversy over same-sex marriage. There are some who would have you believe that homosexuals are bad people who should not have the same rights that everyone else enjoys, even though an objective look at the evidence demonstrates that the vast majority are decent people.

3. Teenage years are a time when we are trying to figure out who we are and where our life is going to go. We tend to seek out others like ourselves and form cliques, each member holding stereotypical views about people in the other cliques. Generally there is tension between these groups based on the judgmental notion that "if you are not like me, you must be bad."

4. Imagine a residential treatment facility for mentally ill adults. There are three shifts: 8 a.m. to 4 p.m., 4 p.m. to 12 a.m., and 12 a.m. to 8 a.m. Every shift thinks it works harder than any other shift. The workers get together and talk about the other shifts. Pretty soon they are regularly coming to the director with complaints about the other shifts. Not only that, but they are using words like lazy, messy, thief, etc. There are also comments about how they look, dress, and act. When I was the director of that facility, I had to take steps to reduce or eliminate the inter-shift tension because it tended to reduce the quality of care our clients received.

I could go on and on, because judgmental thinking is truly something everyone does. However, I wouldn't want you to think, just because we are judgmental based on group membership, that judgmental thinking ends there.

There has been research on Holocaust survivors to identify traits that contributed to their survival. What they found was that those who let go of their moral outrage and judgmental thinking about their situation and faced it with acceptance had a much higher chance of survival. This is an extreme example, but it does illustrate the principle. When something happens that we don't like, we try to reject it. We attach all kinds of labels indicating how bad it is—which is the essence of judgmental thinking.

Here is another example: I was forty years old when my mother died. She was ill for quite a long time before her death. Any objective look at the situation would show that she didn't have much time left. However, in my mind I refused to accept the facts. I believed she would go on and on because the alternative was unthinkable—literally. Even though I knew that we all die at some point, I had labeled my mother's imminent demise as so bad I couldn't even think about it. However, when I saw her dead body in the hospital bed, the reality broke through. It wasn't until I saw her that I felt the pain of loss.

In an instant I felt the pain of loss and realized what I had been doing: living in a state of denial about her true state of health. As a recovering alcoholic I knew that avoiding those "bad" feelings would end badly for me, so I embraced the pain of loss and cried. That acceptance was the beginning of healing. While I still miss her on occasion, I have accepted that she is gone. The pain of loss is much less than it was initially.

Another example: Like most alcoholics, I had this recurring fear that I might be an alcoholic. I would mentally gather evidence to support the idea that I was not an alcoholic. This is because I had judgmental thoughts about alcoholics. If I was an alcoholic, then I was a bad person—in my mind anyway. It wasn't until I shared the fact that I was an alcoholic with a nonjudgmental person that I was able to accept it and drop my judgmental thoughts about alcoholics in general. And, most significantly, it wasn't until I accepted I was an alcoholic that I was able to quit drinking.

Here is a very common example: You are driving in traffic and come up behind someone who is driving five miles under the speed limit, and you can't pass. How often in this situation do you say, "What is wrong with this idiot?" This sounds judgmental. Really, the whole idea behind defensive driving is that other drivers regularly do boneheaded things. We are quick to pass judgment when they do. I catch myself doing it regularly. When I do catch myself, I let go of those judgmental thoughts and direct my attention to the present moment with acceptance. That simple bit of mental gymnastics prevents the cranky mood that otherwise invariably follows some other person's boneheaded driving stunt.

We can have judgmental thoughts about anything. I was trying to teach these principles to my staff when one of them approached me and said, "I thought about it last night and realized I have judgmental thoughts." I told her, "Don't beat yourself up about it. Everybody does." She had to think about it before she could accept that she had judgmental thoughts. I think it is important, when dealing with this subject, to let go of any judgmental thoughts you might have about your own judgmental thoughts.

The "observing your thoughts" exercise described in chapter 2 can be helpful in learning to recognize and release judgmental thoughts.

The second way to cultivate acceptance involves another human being. Human beings are social animals, which means we have *social needs*. One of our most important social needs is *emotional intimacy*. Emotional intimacy means feeling comfortable enough with one or two people in your life to discuss sensitive personal things with them and having reasonable expectation that they will listen with *unconditional acceptance*. When we feel this unconditional acceptance from another person, we are better able to accept ourselves as we are in that moment. By the way, unconditional acceptance doesn't mean that you agree with everything the other person says. You can respectfully disagree. The object is to be aware of and be compassionate about the other person's feelings.

For example, while doing a room search for contraband, one of my staff found several books on Satanism. She was appalled and brought them to me. I talked to the client about it. My thought was that he was looking to summon demons to do his bidding because he felt powerless in his life. I listened to his thoughts on the matter with unconditional acceptance. Then I suggested that there might be more effective ways to develop empowerment and gave him back his books. Interestingly enough, he soon lost interest in demons and started working on his relationships.

Gaining self-acceptance by receiving unconditional acceptance from another person is the principle behind and the reason for the fourth and fifth steps in Alcoholics Anonymous. The fourth step is to perform a thorough moral inventory on yourself. The fifth step is to share it with our Higher Power and *another human being* in hopes that he or she will listen with unconditional acceptance. If you are going to work on yourself, you have to see yourself as you truly are. To do that, you must drop any judgmental thoughts you have about yourself by sharing who you really are with another person. That is the scary part. Sometimes sharing is so scary that people avoid it. Instead they walk around filled with judgmental thoughts about themselves and others, and that poisons their relationships because people tend to get what they give. If you give judgmental thinking, you will get judgmental thinking in return. However, if you want unconditional acceptance, you have to give it.

But why is sharing who you really are so scary? I think we are afraid of being judged—and of being rejected. We all *do* need to feel a sense of belonging, or a connection to other human beings.

Living the mindful lifestyle means constantly noticing when judgmental thoughts arise and releasing them. Face each moment with acceptance.

Chapter 5
Wise Mind

Another concept that is associated with mindfulness practice is the Wise Mind, or the blending of the logical part of the mind with the emotional part. To better understand what is beneficial about this way of thinking, we will examine the individual components.

If we want to be effective in our decision-making, we need to know what factors affect the outcome. In an earlier section we said that effectiveness means playing by "the rules of the universe." Logic tells us about the rules of the universe and allows us to make predictions based on what we have learned that are reasonably accurate. For example, if I drop a rock off a cliff and it falls to the bottom, I can reasonably expect that if I step off the cliff, I will fall to the bottom too. Other past experiences might predict that falling off a cliff would likely be hazardous to my health.

So what's wrong with basing our decisions on logic? For one thing, research has demonstrated that people who have a certain kind of brain injury that prevents them from feeling emotion seem unable to make even simple decisions. They have difficulty deciding what to eat for breakfast or what socks to wear. Clearly emotions are important in our day-to-day life. They tell us about our needs and wants.

Emotions can be pleasurable or painful. Often people will try to avoid the painful emotions and pursue the pleasurable ones. While this may seem like a good idea, and sometimes it is, avoiding painful emotions can interfere with the natural healing process. We need our emotions, even the painful ones. Additionally, acceptance of reality is always healthier than denying it.

So what's wrong with basing our decisions on emotion? While emotions do give us vital information about our internal state, they tell us nothing about the rules of the universe. This is why when people make decisions based primarily on their current emotions, those decisions generally do not bring about the desired result. Those decisions are not effective. Often this type of decision-making is based on wishful thinking or fear.

For example, if you spend more money than you make, you are probably paying attention to your wants and not the reality of your financial situation. People who do this often have other pressing issues that nag at them, and buying stuff makes them feel good for a little while. The same can be said for alcoholism, drug addiction, and other kinds of compulsive behaviors.

How does all this relate to recovery (or to personal growth)? During the course of recovery for most people, there comes a time when they must *act in spite of how they feel*. It has been said that recovery is the hardest, scariest thing a person can do. Recovery involves trying new behaviors and changing old ones. Often this does not feel comfortable. Our emotions tell us to go back to old behavioral patterns even though they haven't worked for us. To advance in our recovery, we must act in spite of how we feel. That is where the Wise Mind comes in. We are aware of our emotions, but our behavior is not dictated by them. We are free to consider what we have learned about the rules of the universe, try new behavioral patterns, and practice new skills until they do feel comfortable.

I like the analogy of the horse and rider. The horse is your emotions and the rider is your logic. Your emotions move you. You can sit on a horse and let that horse go wherever he wants, or you can take the reins wherever *you* want to go. For this arrangement to work, you have to understand and train your horse. In the beginning your horse may not want to go where you want to and refuse, but gentle persistence pays off. Similarly, if you are not used to using the Wise Mind and choosing to act in spite of how you feel, your emotions may balk at not getting their way.

However, with practice you can acknowledge your emotions and still make effective decisions by using logic. You need to listen to what your emotions are telling you, add that to the facts that logic tells you, and then make the decision based on all of it.

There is one more thing I'd like to mention regarding the Wise Mind. There has been an explosion in our knowledge about brain function. We know, for example, that the left hemisphere of the brain deals primarily with logical, mathematical tasks and the right hemisphere deals with emotional, intuitive tasks. We also know that these two connected areas communicate with each other through a bundle of nerve tissue called the corpus callosum. As I mentioned in earlier chapters, mindfulness practices that trigger the relaxation response, such as TM or counting your breath, increase electrical activity in this tissue. This means that the logical part of your brain and the emotional part are talking to each other more than they do in the normal waking state. It stands to reason that regular practice of a deep relaxation type of mindfulness practice will make it easier to use the Wise Mind.

A person living the mindful lifestyle will strive to use the Wise Mind as much as possible. By being fully in present the moment, they will recognize their emotions but not judge them or be ruled by them.

Chapter 6
Willfulness vs. Willingness

Similar to acceptance vs. judgmental thinking is the topic of willfulness vs. willingness. Where judgmental thinking and acceptance apply to specific issues and times, willfulness and willingness apply more to the big picture, to a person's general demeanor or overall philosophy of life.

My guess is that everyone knows or at least has seen what used to be called a "willful child." Or, to put it another way, a spoiled brat. He is that kid you see at the amusement park throwing a fit because he doesn't want to leave when it is time to go home. Perhaps you have seen the teenager who gets mad at the parent who says no and then sneaks out anyway. It is not just children who demonstrate willfulness. Most of us experience a bit of pouting when we don't get our own way—even if it is only internal. I once had an adult client who threatened to pout if he didn't get his way, as if the pouting would be unpleasant for my staff. Fortunately he was bluffing.

Willfulness means setting yourself apart from the universe in an attempt to control or manipulate existence. Many people believe that willfulness is a good thing. We often hear phrases like "stick to your guns," "stay the course," or "my way or the highway." Persistence can be a good thing if you are trying to do something that is difficult but possible based on the reality of the situation. However, often the reality is that we are being persistent based on wishful thinking about something that is not possible based on the reality of the situation.

For example, recovery from an addiction is generally a difficult thing, but we know that many people have put their chemical addiction behind them and gone on to live fulfilling lives. On the other hand, many people do not recover because their actions are based on false beliefs, including:

1.   "I can't do it." Clearly recovery is possible based on the large number of people who have succeeded.

2.   "I don't have a problem." It is interesting to note that people who think this are often miserable but unwilling to acknowledge the reality of their situation because they think that to do so would be painful. The truth is that the problem and the pain are there whether or not we acknowledge them. Only by acknowledging and living through the pain can we put it behind us.

3.   "I can fix it myself." The overwhelming evidence is that social support is an essential component of recovery.

4.   "If I don't talk about my problem, no one will know about it." Generally when we are experiencing symptoms of mental illness or addiction, it is abundantly clear to the people around us.

5.   "I don't deserve the good things in life." This kind of judgmental thinking is often what trips up people who are on the verge of success. The truth is that each person is as deserving as the next. The concept of "deserving" in this context is irrelevant and based not on reality but instead on judgmental thinking.

The interesting thing here is that people often willfully stick to these false beliefs.

The essence of willfulness is this: "I am going to do what I want regardless of what you or anyone else thinks, and if it doesn't turn out like I want, I am going to be upset." The idea is that we can control the universe around us to give us what we want. This idea is false. The truth is that the only thing each of us can control is the individual decisions we make all day, every day. Apparent control over anything other than this is an illusion.

Willingness means readiness to respond wisely and voluntarily as needed. As we all know, life can and does regularly throw all kinds of events at us. Some events are painful, some are pleasurable, and some are neutral. Some events are planned for and controlled by us. Others are unexpected and completely out of our control. Willing people are constantly ready to accept events as they happen. Because their minds are not weighed down by judgmental thinking, they are able to respond more wisely. Responding wisely increases the likelihood that the result will be in line with what we want because we are considering the rules of the universe.

Willingness does *not* mean that you are a pushover. Think of Gandhi. He believed that the British rule of India was wrong. For him, responding wisely meant opposing British rule. He also believed strongly that violence was wrong. Responding wisely meant nonviolent opposition. There can be no doubt that this approach took a great deal of courage—and saved many lives. It was also effective. The British left without a war to push them out. However, to achieve their desired result, Gandhi and his followers had to be willing to accept whatever the British chose to deal out, some of which was very unpleasant.

The willing person is living the mindful lifestyle because he or she must be fully in the present moment to be aware of what is happening and to respond wisely. Willing people use *skillful means* to determine what kind of response is needed, and they are *willing* to accept whatever the universe throws at them.

Chapter 7
Compassion

Let's review what we have said so far. Mindfulness is paying attention to one thing, on purpose, in the present moment. Anything a human being can do can be done in a mindful way. Aspiring to be mindful throughout the day is living the mindful lifestyle. Living the mindful lifestyle means facing each moment with acceptance. An added bonus of this is that you will see things the way they really are—not colored by wishful or judgmental thinking.

One of the things you notice when you see things the way they really are is that human beings are social animals. In fact, you realize that the way to increase your level of acceptance is by experiencing emotional intimacy with others. As you experience emotional intimacy with others, you start to empathize with them. You feel what they feel. When they are happy, you are happy; when they are sad, you are sad. When this happens you are experiencing *compassion*. Compassion means "suffering with." Therefore, the mindful lifestyle is compassionate.

Again, that doesn't mean you are a pushover. As any good parent knows, you have to respond wisely. Just as it is unwise to give children everything they want, sometimes it is unwise to follow the dictates of your compassionate feelings.

When I was running the treatment facility for mentally ill and chemically dependent adults, we had to have rules. We were trying to teach people skills that would help them have better lives. Following the dictates of their emotions was often what landed them in residential treatment. Our Wise Minds told us that the most compassionate thing we could do for our clients was to teach them how to use *their* Wise Minds. However, in this situation it is counterproductive to have only rules and prescribed consequences of violation. There must be compassionate enforcement. We had written into our policies the provision to make exceptions if it was the most compassionate thing to do.

For example, we had a rule against the possession and use of alcohol. Many times clients would go uptown, get drunk, and return to the facility. Our standard response was to send them to detox to sober up. We had the option of discharging them at that time. However, I believed at the time that it was more compassionate to tell them in no uncertain terms that their behavior was wrong, but that we would allow them to return if they agreed to work on their sobriety and to be restricted to the facility for at least a week. This also demonstrated to the client that we were committed to them and their struggle.

Some clients would do this more than once. Some would go on to maintain their sobriety. Others were clearly not interested in recovery. When this became clear to us, the most compassionate thing for us to do was discharge them. One of my staff referred to this as "allowing them to gather more evidence they need to change."

One time we had a client who had been to detox a couple of times. He came to my office and handed me a pint of whiskey. He explained that he had bought it with the intention of getting drunk but had since changed his mind. Even though he had violated the rules by bringing the whiskey to the facility, compassion ruled the day and he suffered no consequence other than being restricted to the facility for a week. He actually thanked me for that because he worried, and rightly so, that he would buy more whiskey. He went on to achieve sobriety.

The point is that even compassion must be tempered with the Wise Mind.

Many recovering alcoholics working the twelve steps get the wrong idea about making amends, even though they are cautioned against it. They push to make amends with people who are hurt more by that effort than if they were simply left alone. Recovering people who do this have not learned the lesson of compassion. They don't consider the feelings of the people with whom they are trying to make amends.

Here is a lesson I learned in compassion from my father. When I was about twelve, we had a couple of young steers that we were raising to butcher. They were in the same pasture as the milk cows. These steers were still being fed milk replacer, something dairy farmers feed calves because it is cheaper than milk. It was my job to feed these two while Dad was milking. I was to take a pailful of milk replacer, let one steer drink half, tap him on the head with a stick so he would pull his head out of the pail, and let the other one finish. This plan actually worked well—until it didn't.

One evening we were doing chores early because we were planning to go to a movie, which we didn't do very often. When I went out to feed the calves, I didn't look for a stick and instead grabbed a hammer that, for reasons unknown to me, was hanging beside the barn door. When I was feeding the first steer, I was daydreaming a bit and he quickly sucked up all the food. As calves will do when they are not happy about something, he butted the pail when it was empty. The corner of the metal bucket hit my shinbone hard. It caught me totally by surprise and hurt a lot. As a reflex I swung the hammer, hitting the calf between his ears. He fell down and rolled down the hill and up against a big tree—stone-cold dead.

I walked the long walk back to the barn to tell Dad. He was milking and some of my nieces and nephews were "helping" him. They were six or seven years old. When I told Dad what had happened, there was a long pause. Then one of my nephews said, "Aren't you going to spank him?" Dad's response was, "I think he has suffered enough already." Even to this day I marvel at the compassion and wisdom of that response from a "simple," uneducated small farmer.

There is one more person I need to mention who needs your compassion: *you.* Don't be so hard on yourself. I suppose that, because compassion refers to how you treat others, it would be more appropriate to use the word "kindness." Most of us are our own worst critics. Be kind to yourself by letting go of the judgmental thoughts you have about yourself. Judgmental thoughts block compassion—be they thoughts about yourself or others.

I believe that people are naturally compassionate (part of being a social animal), and as they work on being less judgmental, their natural compassion comes to the fore.

Therefore, the person living the mindful lifestyle becomes compassionate by practicing acceptance of others.

There are some obstacles to acting with compassion. One is judgmental thinking, as mentioned above. Another is the false belief held by some that compassion would make them less effective—for instance, less competitive in business. I dare say that sometimes that may be true. I think it speaks to the person's values. If you value money or power above all, compassion may interfere with your work. However, if you are like most folks, just trying to get along in this world, nurturing your compassion will enrich your life.

If you want to work directly to cultivate your compassion, there are some exercises you can try. You can sit quietly and direct your attention to feelings of unconditional benevolence while repeating a suitable mantra. One I have seen suggested is: "May all beings find happiness and the causes of happiness and be free from suffering and the causes of suffering." If that seems a little long to you (it does to me), try using just the first half or the second half. Another choice might be to simply use the word "compassion" or any other similar word.

Another similar exercise might be to direct your attention to a specific person. It could even be someone with whom you are having some difficulty. Direct your attention to sending that person unconditional acceptance and compassion. Try to see the world from his or her point of view. Be careful, however, not to get caught up in his or her suffering. The idea is to soothe the person's suffering, not simply to pity him or her. Pity has a judgmental component that actually interferes with the unconditional acceptance necessary for compassion.

I have seen people working in the human services field whose interactions with their clients is tainted by pity, and their judgmental thoughts come through. They usually do not develop good rapport with their clients and are less effective because of it. You may have encountered one of these people—the nurse or doctor who seems to see you as just another body to work on, or the mental health worker who feels sorry for you but doesn't give you credit for being able to make your own decisions. The list goes on.

When I was sixteen I had an accident that involved falling out of a pickup and landing on my butt so hard that I got a concussion. (Please, I've heard all the jokes.) On my first morning in the hospital, I was lying in my bed, dressed only in my underwear, when a group of nurses and orderlies came into my room to change the sheets. Per doctor's orders I was to stay in bed, so I rolled around in my underwear while they changed my sheets and talked about a party they had attended the night before. I think that is the most embarrassed I have ever been. Just a little compassion would have gone a long way in relieving my suffering.

Living the mindful lifestyle means cultivating your compassion and being willing to be of service to others.

Human beings the world over are more alike than they are different. I wonder how the world would change if each of us exercised more compassion in our dealings with those we came into contact with.

Chapter 8
Gratitude

I want to move the discussion to the topic of gratitude as a mindfulness practice. Gratitude is that mental state that acknowledges receipt of something from an individual or the universe at large that is of benefit to you or that you find pleasant or helpful. It can be quite easy when you have had a difficult life to spend time thinking about all the bad things that happened. This is human nature. It is also human nature to feel bad when we think about those bad things. This can keep us mired in negativity. However, if a person gets in the habit of looking for things to feel gratitude for, it is easier to let go of the negative thinking, which will at the very least make you feel better about your life. It may even open your eyes to more opportunities that negative thinking blinded you to.

Another way to look at it is in the context of willingness vs. willfulness. Willful people do not feel gratitude. They believe that whatever they receive is because they can somehow control the universe and make it give them what they want. They might feel a sense of accomplishment when they get what they want or like and rage when they don't. Willing people do not have expectations because they are living in the present, but they are open to whatever the universe provides and feel gratitude when the good things come.

Gratitude is related to compassion because an act of compassion requires at least two people. One person performs the act of compassion and the other is the recipient. If the recipient is not burdened with a sense of entitlement, he or she will experience gratitude. Of course, many times a person receives something and there is no obvious giver—or you could say the universe is the giver. Whether or not the universe can experience compassion is a question I will leave up to you to answer. I think it does.

Here's an example: A week or so ago, I found a dollar lying on the floor at our local Walmart. Realistically, there was no way to find the owner, so I picked it up and said "thank you" to the universe.

Another example: Most hunter-gatherer cultures, such as the Native Americans, would thank the spirits of the animals they killed for giving their lives so their people could eat. Most of us in our modern technological society have lost this connection. When we are hungry, we eat. We have a sense of entitlement about it even though many people cannot take for granted that they will have enough to eat.

When I was teaching mindfulness to my mentally ill and chemically dependent clients, we talked about gratitude in the context of recovery. The idea was that, because you can only think about one thing at a time, if you look for good things to feel gratitude for, there isn't room in your conscious awareness to think about all the things that are wrong with your life. Many students found it helpful in their recovery.

A good way to get in the habit is to set aside a few minutes every day to acknowledge the good things you have received that day. Or you could simply go through each day with the intent to acknowledge and be thankful for the good things as they happen. As this becomes habit, most people find that their mood improves and their relationships improve because they become less demanding.

A nice bonus of feeling gratitude is that it often it leads to action. Sometimes we like to pay back. This can strengthen social bonds and even motivate a person to choose a career or write a book about recovery or mindfulness.

Living the mindful lifestyle means living each day with the intent to notice the good things and feel gratitude.

Chapter 9
Gifts of the Spirit

The previous chapters represent the bulk of what is becoming "mainstream" mindfulness. What I am going to talk about here may sound a little weird to you. There are many people who use these techniques and believe they work. There is even some scientific evidence that some of these techniques are effective. I am talking about the idea that through meditation you can achieve tangible results in the "real" world. I'm talking about things like faster, more effective studying, enhanced problem solving, finding lost items, curing physical illness, attracting things like wealth and love, and increasing or developing extrasensory abilities like remote viewing or more powerful intuition.

I will ask you to keep an open mind here. I include these practices because they fit the mindfulness definition of directing your attention to one thing. In addition, they have been part of my experience with mindfulness, and I believe I benefit from using them.

The first example I will talk about is called the Silva Mind Control Method. It was first developed in the 1950s by Jose Silva, who founded an organization to teach his methods that still exists today. He also wrote a book, *The Silva Mind Control Method*, which is still in print and available online.

Silva talks about various "levels" of the mind. What he is referring to is the electrical activity in the brain as measured by an electroencephalograph. The document produced by this machine is called an electroencephalogram (EEG). It actually looks like a bunch of wavy lines on a piece of paper. Research in this area indicates that different wavelengths or frequencies (cycles per second, or CPS) correspond to different states of consciousness. There are four basic categories, each designated with a letter from the Greek alphabet. Frequencies of 14 CPS and higher correspond to a normal waking state and are designated beta. Frequencies of 7 to 14 CPS are designated as alpha and correspond to a light meditative state but are also noted in light sleep. Frequencies between 4 and 7 CPS are designated theta and correspond to a deeper meditative state, and also deeper sleep. Frequencies below 4 CPS are designated delta and generally correspond to deep sleep.

Silva refers to the beta state as the "outer consciousness." He refers to the alpha state as the "inner consciousness." His contention is that we all can access powers in the alpha state that we cannot in the beta state. There is actually quite a bit of documentation dating back to the 1970s that this is true.

Silva offers a training course that starts by teaching people to access their alpha state at will. He suggests counting backward to relax. There are also suggestions to go to your "lower levels of mind." Here he is referring to the alpha state. The idea is to be deeply relaxed. If this sounds like hypnosis to you, pat yourself on the back. Silva actually started his research with self-hypnosis.

Once people are in the alpha state, they perform mental tasks, including mentally projecting objects on a screen (also in their minds). This exercise is intended to improve the ability to visualize things in your mind. Once this is accomplished, people are asked to visualize on their "screens" situations in their lives they would like to change. Then they are asked to visualize what would replace those situations. They push the old out with the new from left to right. The idea is that the mind will manifest the new situation. It is not enough to simply want something in the beta state; people have to use the "power" of the alpha state to get results.

Once students become proficient at this, they move on to other things, including:

- Projecting their awareness outside their bodies to locate lost objects
- Using this expanded awareness to diagnose illness in themselves and others and even to provide treatment
- Contacting "spirit guides" for guidance
- Improving their memory
- Communicating with others through telepathy
- Improving their intuition about future events

Gary Green

As you can see, some of these claims are quite remarkable. There is a fair amount of anecdotal evidence that this actually works. The Silva organization, or Silva Life System, website includes some research documentation as well as free lessons.

Before you decide to go wild trying to manifest all kinds of fabulous things this way, you should know that there are rules:

1. You must desire the thing you are trying to manifest. You can't manifest some goofy thing just to see if it works.
2. It must be something you believe can happen.
3. You must expect it to happen.
4. You can do no harm. If you are mad at someone and trying to cause that person harm, it won't work.

When I read these rules, I am reminded of Jesus talking about miracles: "Oh, ye of little faith." To perform a miracle his disciples had to want it to happen, believe it could happen, and expect it to happen. They had to have faith. "With faith you can move mountains."

Regarding the harm issue, Silva says that in alpha you are in contact with a Higher Intelligence that actually prevents harm. The worst that can happen is that it just won't work.

According to Silva, as you practice going into the alpha state, you start experiencing it throughout the day without trying. This reminds me of the notion that you can be mindful as you move through your daily routine. Silva also has a trick to enable a person to access the "power of alpha" throughout the day. He calls it the "three finger method."

First you have to prepare by going into alpha. Then place the tips of your first two fingers on either hand on the tip of your thumb, forming a circle. Then suggest internally to yourself that when you need to be in alpha, you can touch these fingers to your thumb and will immediately be in the alpha state. When you can't remember someone's name, for example, touch your fingers to your thumb, close your eyes, and see it on your mental screen. I have tried this with some success.

I have also tried going into the alpha state before studying. Whenever I did this I got good grades on the tests. I realize this is just anecdotal evidence, but it convinced me.

Another technique suggests that you can enter the alpha state before going to sleep (you do this naturally anyway) and ask for guidance in a dream. There are actually several well-documented cases of people receiving guidance this way. For example, Elias Howe, the inventor of the sewing machine, had reached an impasse in his work to develop a successful sewing machine. Then he had a dream in which he was being chased by angry natives with spears that had holes near the tips. When he woke up he knew the answer. He had to put the hole in the tip of the needle to make the sewing machine work.

Silva also states that better health originates in the mind. He gives two reasons for this:

1. You can only think about one thing at a time.
2. When you concentrate on a thought, the thought becomes real because your body transforms it into action.

His suggestion to unlock the body's healing potential is to use the following mantra: "Day by day, in every way, I am getting better and better." He goes on to say that, because in the alpha state words have more impact, you can go into your alpha state and say only once, "Day by day, in every way, I am getting better, better, and better." This will get you the same result. He added, "Negative thoughts and negative suggestions have no effect on me at any level of mind"—just to be sure.

He lists six steps to self-healing:

1. You must begin in the beta state. You must feel yourself becoming a more loving and forgiving person. Try to see unconditional love and acceptance as an end in itself. This reminds me of the kind of personal growth I talked about in my first book, *In Pursuit of Joy*, as well as in previous chapters of this book. This is going to take some effort on your part.
2. Go into the alpha state.

3. Mentally talk to yourself about step 1. Visualize yourself as a loving, compassionate person who greets each moment with acceptance.

4. Briefly visualize and experience the illness mentally to focus your healing energy.

5. Quickly erase this mental image and replace it with the image of yourself completely cured. Linger over this image, feel it, and know you deserve it.

6. Mentally return to step 1 and end by repeating, "Every day and in every way, I am getting better, better, and better."

Let's examine this process. Essentially Silva is saying that becoming a more loving, accepting person is good for you. Additionally, half of the steps are essentially the same—work on becoming a more loving, accepting person. Then he uses the same visualization process he uses for other things. While it isn't stated explicitly, it is clear that the four rules mentioned earlier in this chapter apply. With faith you can move mountains.

Another aspect of the Silva Method is the mental workshop. This is a safe place filled with all the tools and equipment needed to do all kinds of things. It is in this workshop that much of the alpha work is done.

When setting up their mental workshop, Silva students visualize two assistants—a man and a woman. The interesting thing about the assistants is that apparently every student starts the session with a firm idea of whom they want as assistants, but they almost always get someone else. Does this mean that these assistants or guides are actually a separate entity, or do they just represent a projection from our subconscious mind? I honestly do not know, so I will leave it to you to answer that question for yourself.

I have tried some of these things and have gotten some interesting results. For example, when I was in my early twenties, I was out drinking and fell down a full flight of stairs onto the concrete basement floor of a bar. I later learned that I had cracked two vertebrae. However, at the time I had no medical insurance (this was pre-Obamacare), so I didn't go to a doctor. I also didn't miss a day of work. I was working at the time as the foreman in a welding and fabrication shop. I usually worked ten-hour days. So how did I do it?

During this period of my life, I had been doing TM for several years. I had also read a book called *The Power of Alpha Thinking* by Jess Stearn, who completed the Silva Mind Control training and wrote this book about his experience. I had been experimenting with some of the techniques before my injury.

I will tell you that cracked vertebrae are very painful—especially if you are walking around on a concrete floor all day. Looking back at that time, I realize that part of my coping strategy was that I accepted the pain and just got on with my day. However, there were times when the pain became unbearable. I did not use pain medication; instead I used alpha thinking. When the pain became unbearable, I would find a relatively quiet place where I could sit for five minutes or so and go into my alpha state. I would visualize the pain in my back. It looked red and inflamed. Then I would visualize a golden healing energy being pushed into the area by someone's hands. As I did this, my back would start to hurt less. Then I would visualize the area as pink and healthy. Within five minutes I was able to go back to work.

I realize that with back injuries, the muscles around the injury tend to tense up. This can put pressure on the injured area and even pinch nerves. In my case, as the pain got worse my right leg would start to hurt, I think because of a nerve pinching. As the pain got worse, the muscle tension would increase in a vicious cycle. The deep relaxation of the alpha thinking would relax the muscles and lessen this secondary pain. I believe that this practice helped heal my back faster.

So how does all this alpha thinking fit into the big picture of mindfulness?

1. I believe it is a mindfulness practice because it fits into the basic definition of directing your attention to one thing.

2. Additionally, the underlying philosophy of personal growth and compassion also fits well with the mindful lifestyle.

3. The information about the different frequencies of brain

waves actually fits in with research about other mindfulness practices such as TM.

4. You might think that visualizing the future you want is not living in the present moment. I beg to differ. If you have a broken car, you can fix it in a mindful way, staying in the present as you make each repair until the car is how you want it. Similarly, if you have a broken life, you can work on fixing it in a mindful way even if that work involves visualizing the future.

5. It seems as though the main thing that interferes with being able to do the remarkable things Silva talks about is judgmental thinking about the possibility of making "miracles."

While doing the research for this book, I found a lot of different systems very similar to Silva's. Most of these systems have a book or two dedicated to them. Some have organizations that offer classes. However, Silva's organization appears to be the largest and most effective.

There is one other type of mental/psychic practice that I should mention before I end this chapter. Most people, I think, have heard of Edgar Cayce. For those of you who haven't, he was a "psychic" who lived from 1877 to 1945. He could enter into a trancelike meditative state and answer questions asked by another person, usually his wife. These questions could be about anything, including diagnosing health problems and prescribing treatments that were generally quite effective. Called by some the "Sleeping Prophet," he was apparently able to tap into some kind of all-encompassing information source. His "readings" covered almost every topic. He was able to answer questions about historical events going back thousands of years. He was also allegedly able to answer questions about the future with remarkable accuracy.

These "readings" are all very well documented and cataloged at the Association for Research and Enlightenment (ARE) in Virginia Beach, Virginia. The association has a very interesting website.

Cayce died in 1945. His life was remarkable enough on its own. Many people believe we were very lucky to have had such a remarkable talent among us.

Then along came Ross Peterson, who appeared to have the same abilities as Cayce. At first glance Peterson seemed to be an unlikely candidate for a prophet or any other kind of spiritual leader. He struggled with alcoholism, obesity, relationship difficulties (seven marriages), and other issues. Yet during his recovery process, he progressed in his spiritual development to the point where he could imitate Cayce. The accuracy of his readings is well documented. Interestingly, Cayce himself believed that anyone could learn to do what he did. Peterson believed that meditation was essential to the process. He even started a school to teach his methods to others.

A quick Internet search reveals that there are currently several people who appear to exhibit the same ability. During a reading these people are purportedly operating in the delta (slowest) brain wave band. The conscious mind appears to be suppressed, because all these people need a helper or guide to ask the questions and record the answers. It is interesting to me that all these people believe that a life of compassion, unconditional acceptance, and regular meditation is necessary to reach the point of spiritual development where these things are possible.

I have including this information because it indicates the true depth of the human mind and the amazing "gifts of the spirit" available to us all.

Certainly there is a place for this kind of mental work in the mindful lifestyle.

Chapter 10
Bringing It All Together

Even though this is a short book, there is a lot of information in it. Let's put it all together and try to come up with a plan to move into the mindful lifestyle and start reaping all the benefits I talked about in the preface and more.

Where should a person start? I would recommend starting with a deep relaxation practice such as TM or counting your breath. Find time to do at least one session every day for at least ten minutes. (Twenty would be better.) I suggest you try to fit in this session in the morning, even if you have to get up a bit earlier. Start with one session in the morning, every morning. If you have a convenient time to do a second session later in the day—when you get home from work, for example—do so. Remember to notice thoughts that pop up and then direct your attention back to your chosen mindfulness practice. If you consistently fall asleep when you meditate, adjust your sleep habits and work on your sleep hygiene until you can meditate without falling asleep. This may take a couple of weeks.

During this time try to remember to direct your attention to what you happen to be doing at the time. As you practice this, it will become habit.

When you are able to meditate consistently, add a brief prayer of thanks either at the beginning or the end of your meditation sessions. Don't just give it lip service. Really give thanks to the universe for things you genuinely feel grateful for, and try to remember throughout the day to notice those things. You will remember these when you meditate.

When this becomes habit, add a statement to your gratitude, like "Day by day, in every way, I am getting better, better, and better." Perhaps you could also add something like "I am becoming a more compassionate person." Remember that by recognizing and releasing your judgmental thoughts, you will become more compassionate.

At this point you will be meditating at least once a day, trying to be fully present in each moment and cultivating your gratitude and compassion. One more thing to remember as you go through your day: when things happen that trigger a strong emotional reaction, pause and call upon your logic. Use your Wise Mind. You are now living the mindful lifestyle. You will see changes in your life. You will be more relaxed, less reactive, and less stressed. You will be more effective in your decisions and generally feel better about life. You will become more willing to accept what life throws at you. You will be healthier both physically and mentally, and you will live longer. Congratulations!

This may be as far as you want to take it, and that's okay. But you may want to take things further. Learn more about the Silva Method—or even take it all the way and become a "sleeping prophet." You are as deserving as anyone else of all the gifts the universe has to offer. Enjoy. May you find all the peace and joy the universe has to offer.

Review Requested:
If you loved this book, would you please provide a review at Amazon.com?

CPSIA information can be obtained
at www.ICGtesting.com
Printed in the USA
FFOW04n0438260215
11281FF

9 781631 357008